Necessary Clearings

JENNIFER CLARK

Necessary Clearings

Copyright © 2014 by Jennifer Clark

All rights reserved. No part of this book may be reproduced or transmitted in any form or by any means without written permission of the author.

ISBN: 9780985315146
Library of Congress Control Number: 2013942707

Cover art: "The Great Northern Spoon Swan" by John Sokol

Published by Shabda Press
Pasadena, CA 91107

To my son, Tom

Acknowledgments

"Signs of a Weakening Economy" appeared in *Rose & Thorn Journal*.

"Because It's Difficult to Hear Liquid Voice Above the Loud Buzz of Day" appeared in *Driftwood Magazine*.

"Scrotum Humanum" appeared in *Defenestration*.

"Territorial Markings" appeared in *Main Street Rag*.

"Sweetwater's Donut Mill," "Minutes into a Three Hour Journey," and "A Brief Notion in the Evolution of Avian Migration" appeared in *Encore Magazine*. "Minutes into a Three Hour Journey" also anthologized in *Longest Hours* (Silver Boomer Books).

"Breakfast Mourning" and "Osteonecrosis" appeared in *Pain and Memory*, Editions Bibliotekos. "Breakfast Mourning" received nomination for a Pushcart Prize.

"Saturday Syntax: American Goldfinch Style" and "In the Downpour of Your Absence" appeared in *The Midwest Quarterly*. "In the Downpour of Your Absence" later published in *Poemeleon*.

"Spring Thaw" appeared in *Kalamazoo Gazette* and received honorable mention in adult poetry category for 2011 Kalamazoo Gazette Literary Award.

"Exporting the Dead" appeared in *Complex Allegiances*, Universal Table/ Wising Up Press.

"Snake Wife," "What the Balloon Saw," and "Interim Problem Report II9V-0880" appeared in *Paper Crow*. "Snake Wife" made Ellen Datlow's Honorable Mention List for "Best Horror of the Year-2011." "Interim Problem Report 119V-0880" nominated for a 2014 Rhysling Award.

"Where is Norman Rockwell When You Need Him?" appeared in *Centrifugal Eye*.

"At a Crossroads in Japan" appeared in *Raven Chronicles*.

"The Offender Recalls the First Time" appeared in *Gloom Cupboard*.

"Lives Overlapped" appeared in *Dogs Singing: A Tribute Anthology*, Salmon Press.

"Upon Attending the Unveiling of Galaxy Messier 101" appeared in *Astropoetica*.

"Apology to the Grayling" appeared in *Pear Noir!*.

"Grieving the God of My Youth" (part I) and "I Want a Church" appeared in *Windhover*.

"What I Wanted to Say" and "The Molting Season" appeared in *You are here: The Journal of Creative Geography at the University of Arizona*, "Suspensions: Spaces Between Illness and Health."

"Laryngitis" and "Uncle Ernie's Pancake House, Labor Day" appeared in *Solo Novo, 122 Days*.

"Making Raspberries" appeared in *All Poetry Is Prayer*, a FIRE anthology.

"Gay in the Age of Copper" appeared in *failbetter*.

Special thanks to

Jane Mayes and Donna Carroll, your suggestions and keen eyes helped me hone many of these poems

and Teresa Mei Chuc, for believing in my poems

Contents

Signs of a Weakening Economy 1
Because It's Hard To Hear Liquid Voice Above the Loud Buzz of Day.... 3
Scrotum Humanum 4
Territorial Markings 5
A Visit to Kairos 6
Sweetwater's Donut Mill 7
When Your Father Dies, I Will Fail to Comfort You 9
Breakfast Mourning 10
Saturday Syntax: American Goldfinch Style 11
Osteonecrosis 12
Portrait of the Artist 13
Spring Thaw 14
Exporting the Dead 16
Snake Wife 18
Where is Norman Rockwell When You Need Him? 19
Minutes into a Three Hour Journey 21
Wedding Anniversary, July 2010: Peru, Indiana 23
Solo Act 25
At a Crossroads in Japan 27

From a Second Floor Verandah in Naples, Florida 28
The Offender Recalls the First Time 29
Charleston's Circle Church Graveyard in Early March. 31
The Neighbors Behind Me and Two Doors Down. 32
Lives Overlapped 34
Etymological Swim 35
Upon Attending the Unveiling of Galaxy Messier 101 36
Apology to the Grayling. 38
The Hard Ones' Response 41
Interim Problem Report 119V-0080. 42
I Find Myself 45
Allied in Spring 47
Allied in Summer. 49
Grieving the God of My Youth 50
I Want a Church 53
What I Wanted to Say 55
Even Heaven Will Not Be Like This 58
Laryngitis. 59
Making Raspberries 61
Gay in the Age of Copper 62
What the Balloon Saw 64
In The Downpour of Your Absence 66
In Trying to Find a Home for Your Jewelry 67
Uncle Ernie's Pancake House, Labor Day. 68
In This Time of Drought a Silver Lining 70
The Molting Season 71
Genealogy Goes Both Ways on Park Street 73
A Brief Notion in the Evolution of Avian Migration 75

Signs of a Weakening Economy

Consider the child who,
now that he has had
a taste of silver
wishes away more teeth,

has, at the age of five
settled upon a career
that requires giving up
pieces of himself, entails

twirling wobbly whites
'til pink strands release
the tiny dancers upon
his hand. Call him a

professional
tooth trader
pearly white picker
under the pillow pusher

this silver dollar taker
woos enchanting fairies by
offering up hard
slivers of belief.

Soon enough he will
take leave of splendid space,
where infinitesimal wings
stir eyelashes and dreams,

and enter into
this place in which
the only hand that slips
money under the pillow is you.

Because It's Hard To Hear Liquid Voice Above the Loud Buzz of Day

I've been dreaming
        about water lately.

The first time, my son and I were in a meadow
gathering shards of blues and greens. They clattered
against enamel innards of pails; handles
hooked over our arms—like how old ladies
hold their oversized, vinyl purses.
Mommy, I think this is the last rainbow.

The final one leaks into waking hours.
I was a sparrow, thirsty, frantically
searching and then I saw it: water—the size of
a pillow—shimmering, roped off
like a museum exhibit, surrounded by men
with guns. When I awoke

I knew that
the water is leaving us.

Scrotum Humanum

In 1676, because
he did not doubt
the greatness of
man, Robert Plot

mistook that which
remained—the knee
end of a thigh bone
of Megalosaurus—for

fossilized balls
that once swayed
between steely thighs
of giant man. Perhaps

he doubted the wisdom
of a God who would create
massive creatures only to
allow them to disappear,

chose, instead, to hunker
beneath the shadow of a
God who shrunk the
thundering balls of man.

Researchers have found that the presence of stickers and decals—regardless of the message—on a vehicle predicts the tendency to be an aggressive driver. Szlemko, W. J., Benfield, J. A., Bell, P. A., Deffenbacher, J. L. and Troup, L. (2008), Territorial Markings as a Predictor of Driver Aggression and Road Rage. Journal of Applied Social Psychology, 38: 1664–1688.

Territorial Markings

When the white van woman
cuts you off in traffic, just be
prepared: *if you want to ride her ass
you better be pulling her hair.* Speaking
of ass—even though she's a
coffee lover—hers is dragging, slapped silly
by burning beliefs and too much *coexis*ting.

She wags her steely rear in your face, insists
you *normalize breastfeeding by nursing in public.*
You almost feel sorry for her as, instead of
driving her *honor roll student* to school
she'd *rather be getting a tattoo* to compliment
the almost invisible heart on her right hip.
This one-way relationship, in which she
cares to know nothing of you, is grating.

Even after she has disappeared,
swallowed up by the sea of traffic
you see her hands grip the steering wheel
a little tighter, realize she only wants
to be remembered, to make her mark.

A Visit to Kairos

Favorite nightgown—
a profusion of blue
roses in full bloom.

Your hand, a petal,
sinks into mine
and sighs. You whisper

I am not afraid.
Only my eyes reply for
I am not as sure—

like a dandelion
gone   to   seed
pieces of you

set out,
spreading far   and   wide
leaving us

here, wandering
in a field of
fading cotton.

Sweetwater's Donut Mill

(Sprinkle Road, Kalamazoo, MI)

Remember that coupon you pressed into my hand?
Good for free dozen donut holes! it said.
Almost a year to the day
your lost offering fluttered down
from the kitchen cabinet, crumpled but still here.

We miss your monthly invitations for lunch.
Ice water in jelly glasses, a tidy side salad,
homemade dinner rolls, hearty main course,
dessert with coffee.

Don't clean up, you'd chide.
*It will give me something
to do once you are gone.*

Over donut holes,
my coffee,
his chocolate milk,
my son toasts you.

His chocolate and sugar
rimmed lips pronounce:
*These donuts are sooo good
they must grow them here.*

I laugh for all of us,
at the image unfurling behind
Sweetwater's parking lot—
a thick cord of donut holes rising up

clinging to swollen stems like
glazed Brussels sprouts
powdered by God's own hand.

When Your Father Dies, I Will Fail to Comfort You

When your father dies, I will fail to comfort you.

As you talk into the phone, your face glistening,
a few of my words will fall upon the flowered cloth
you've washed and ironed and snapped smartly
over the kitchen table.
You are the salt of the earth.
I will say or think this. Not sure which.
Not sure why.

I will not know this moment, for
when my husband dies, I will not be here.
As you listen to the voice in the phone, you will watch
my finger trace the outline of cotton flowers.
You shall not hear my soul rumble
against this shell, my body.
The skin holds on. Remember that.

It will not occur to me to squeeze
between these ribbed bars
and escape this body I do not know,
in which the heart does not spasm,
but remains quiet,
still,
beating.

Until release comes, I will fail to comfort you.

Breakfast Mourning

Pulling the bag of frozen blueberries
out of the freezer, I think of Pete.

These berries came into their fullness
just as he began to slip away.

These berries, blue skins frozen in time,
delicate casings thawing to the breath of morning.

In their new, thickly battered home they speak
snapping, sizzling, recalling visions of their former selves.

At my feet, my son bangs lids and pots together in glee
as I flip a pancake.

In the heart of summer, we visited him.
His voice raspy in a withering body.

We left that day not knowing what to do and so we
drove around the countryside.

We stopped at Leduc's Farm and
bought ten pounds of freshly picked blueberries.

One pie and batch of muffins later, he was gone.
Left his wife and children and grandchildren and countless friends.

My son inhales his pancake, brilliant splashes of blue
disappearing with each bite.

Saturday Syntax: American Goldfinch Style

Window glass rattles,
interrupting morning's silent flow.
Dashing outside, we see,
curled slightly, a yellow comma
punctuating the brown porch.

Dark wings—
two slender parentheses
hug a hollow body
wrapped in gold.

We pause, our bodies
remembering to breathe
as we gaze upon the tiny finch.
A flight ended in mid-sentence.

Osteonecrosis

Her bones are leaving her.

This home that she was born into
is falling down around her,

sockets and joints disintegrating—
first the hips, then the shoulders crumble.

She stands amidst the ruins; dusty bones,
like time, slip through her fingers.

Blood and dreams and fears
exposed to the elements and

to doctors with shiny instruments
who help her, bone by bone to replace herself.

First hips, then shoulders, now the right knee.
She begs someone to feed her dying bones.

The ankles grow weak,
collapse is imminent.

Another bone is leaving her.

Portrait of the Artist

Let the rains fall, for we are sheltered. The paint has long dried
on his precise, no-mistake women who flaunt juicy melon bottoms
and bursting, olive-shaped nipples, who wear
shoulder blades crisp as the letter j, one forward and one backward,
while his men–unworthy of paint–sit on islands of India ink,
shirtless and unshaven,
slumped over spent bottles of liquor, faces shrouded by wide-brimmed hats.

He is wearing, even in summer, the same blue knit hat and windbreaker
he wore last winter when we first met.
He does not trust the noon sea of shirts and ties.
One hand grips his latest work, a cardboard sign; shades of reds and oranges
meticulously announcing: *Help the needy–contributions welcome!*

Over two coffees and three cigarettes he speaks of AA for alcoholism,
Librium for manic depression, prescription pills for chronic back pain,
new and improved, he says, a little too loudly,
convincing himself he's changed.

I've been here too long, he sighs and stands to leave, but not before kissing me.
I let him this time. His words, *Help the needy–contributions welcome!*
sandwiched between the bread of our warm bodies as his mouth
paints a wet, smokey ring 'round my lips. He abandons the soup
which can not possibly ease his hunger and leaves the shelter of the deli.
In two weeks time, his heart will abandon him. He will leave this world
and all his men, forever stumbling towards paradise.

Spring Thaw

(for Nancy)

She went down into the basement wanting
walnuts and discovered a dead freezer. To
salvage what she could, she folded herself

over the rim of silent lips and dove into
the past.   Jeaned legs slice through
dank air as her arms wade through bloated bodies

of vegetables, hunks of unidentified meat, and
other sundry items to find walnuts to sprinkle
on her dinner salad.

When she reaches the bottom—a small pool now—
the wedding cake, smartly bundled in plastic, is
there to greet her, slogging about on lasagna skis,
two well-hydrated noodles. *Slimy buggers,* she thinks.

She has to laugh—that he'd gone to the trouble
of covering the cardboard box in plastic before
burying the top cake in this forgotten haystack.

She unravels time, recalls how he sucked with a
red straw the air right out between layers of plastic,
thinks how funny memory is, that one could
remember the color of straw held between

an ex-husband's lips, could recall the sweet taste
of promise: Bavarian cream with raspberry preserves
and yet, a middle name could slip one's mind.
What had his been? Anthony? No. It was Marshall.
Maybe.

If he'd wrapped their marriage in this much care
it might not have grown stale in a matter of months.
Hugging the softened cake to her belly, she slides
her back down the freezer, thinks it might be

Gerald, Jim or Justin? A "j" sound
rings a bell. Her hand the fork
she lifts a clot of thawed cake to mouth.

Despite what's-his-middle-name's best efforts
the past mumbles of broccoli, chicken,
crackles with cold and time,
here now on her ripened tongue
tasting of everything but walnuts.

Every year, the corpses of hundreds of immigrants are flown from San Francisco to their home countries.

—San Francisco Weekly, Lauren Smiley, January 20, 2009

Exporting the Dead

When an elephant dies
bones rest and relatives remember;
wrinkled trunks inhale the scent of skull,
then silently caress ivory tusks.
Massive feet rise, and soft
as a whisper, stroke that which remains.

When a human—deemed illegal—dies
the good death begins; it is in
the business of 'international transfers'
that a life no longer, is legitimized.
Documents once withheld
made up for now, an offering
of papers—presented to the corpse—
certified and sealed, pinned to
that which remains, like a
note from a guilty parent:
we withhold love no longer.

It costs more to fly dead
than alive, even though the dead
don't ask for pillows.
In this sport of exporting
we pretend they're alive.

So when a human dies illegal
bones fly home
or glide on the backs of waves
to Mexico, Nicaragua, El Salvador
for singing relatives to bury.
A mother folds her arms and hugs herself.
A sea of feet stand above blanketed bones
and remember that their dead once lived.

Snake Wife

Skin so tight now,
every breath, a chore.
She is not sure how she
stepped into this skin that
once glistened and grooved.

She rattles against the silverware
drawer, drags her dulled self across
the cool countertop, presses against
the Kenmore dishwasher; relief comes

as the can opener catches her throat and
peels her skin from head to toe.
Cloudy eyes clear as she stands raw
and shiny before the toaster.

She picks up the crumpled life, coiled at her feet
and arranges this husk of a woman
—only a prop now—
on the living room couch.

Biding her time
while things appear to be in their place.
Soon she will slip out into the damp
of night, never to return.

He will think she is only hiding.
With a stick, he will pound the
granite jungle and find only moonlight
melting onto papery skin.

Where is Norman Rockwell When You Need Him?

Against a sprawling canvas
bordered by cornfields tinged with copper,
my husband and his family stand still as stalks in this wide, open place.
Just our boy moves in this Indiana heat. Crouched in our circle of shade,
he picks up a stone, only to drop one for another.

"Why it's Wilson and Kate!" shouts my mother-in-law, who spots
them first. She clasps her hands in delight, as if these neighbors
from just down the road lived light years away.
Stones spit out tired complaints as a burnt umber Plymouth
rolls slowly up the drive. Dust cloaks its dry greeting
over the scene. When it wearies, you can see

that we stand in this painting not yet painted,
the peeling barn hugged by a cerulean sky, the old
farmer and his wife polite as pie. A small smile dances upon his lips,
then leaps across to hers, then back again. Paint them shiny. Like tiny stars
dropped from the sky they burn bright. Wilson wears denim overalls
and holds a present wrapped in plain brown paper. Look closely

at his hands, two small planets of rugged terrain. Dip
your brush into a lifetime thick of sun and earth.
Kate stands beside him in a yellow ochre dress. Pencil in
peonies, then use a clean, dry brush with
just a touch of watery white to give a hint of flowers.

"I hear you like flags," he winks to our boy as his hands bestow the gift.
Kate leans in and whispers in my ear, "He made it himself." Bathe their
pleasant mixing of voice in a sea of swirling pigments.

I stand beside my husband, sprung from this Indiana ground. Sketch him
solid, warm, stretching for miles. Can you see our boy release
crumpled paper to the wind, pull the wooden flag to his chest?

A car with blurry occupants rushes by.
Get this moment down so that we and the hurried ones
of this world may pass through once again and see

plain brown wrappings tumbling out of view,
the gift opened,
readied for the embrace.

Minutes into a Three Hour Journey

Are we there yet?
our son asks as
the car window frames

row upon row of
cornstalks the color of sand.
Like bitter fingers

they poke through
hardened earth
bent and hollow now,

having given up months ago
plump, baby kernels
nestled in fine silk.

Are we there yet?

Still, rows flicker by.
Snow like spilled diamonds
glitters amongst the broken

husks of hands that
hold nothing but time, barely
rustling the same story.

Are we there yet?

Perhaps we are.
Let us stop
for a moment,

jump over barbed-wire fencing
and run with abandon.
Let us say we are here.

Wedding Anniversary, July 2010: Peru, Indiana

In the Circus Capital of the world
under the Big Top, eyes focus on the tightrope
as our six year wedding anniversary slips away
without benefit of card or kiss.

In the car, sweat dries, clings to us like salty pearls.
Our son and his friend—rejuvenated by snow cones—
hold their "magic wands." Like miniature disco balls
they shimmer and spin above our heads.

As we travel to your parents' home, dust rises
to greet us, cornfields wave their tasseled heads
and soybeans clap their soft green hands.
In honor of us, I like to think.

That evening, with the spine of your
Maconaquah High School senior yearbook
nestled between her creamy thighs, your wife
will wait for you to come to bed.

Her fingertips will roam back in time
to float above your smiling eyes,
caress your fuzzy "moustache"
and brush your polyestered arms.

Would your eighteen-year old self
—with his whole life stretched before him—
have imagined being cradled in the soft belly of this middle aged woman
sensibly clad in high brief, white cotton underwear and gown?

She will press hard her index finger against valedictorian lips
that twenty eight years later, in full color
will question the wisdom of sharing a straw
and risk catching his hacking cough.

She will ignore the protests and sip with abandon from his Lemon Squeeze,
wanting to share something besides this sweltering day.
At the thought of her, this older woman loving you,
would you have shuddered in delight?

Solo Act

Too old to shovel
but he can't bear
for one more minute
to be battered about by
memories, warm and fluid,
surging over him, pinning him down
in this house that no longer holds his wife.

He bundles himself up
for heaven's sake put on your galoshes, she'd say,
reaches for the pale yellow broom
—she had put it there last, leaned it
against the corner of the kitchen—
holds it to his chest and
steps out into hush of morning.
Snowflakes as flat as pennies
fall without a sound.

Under an endless sky
he sweeps the snow.
Shuffling down the drive
lined with trees the color of coffee
he finds temporary relief
as memories huddle together for warmth
into a lump at the base of his heart.

From across the street—
effortlessly balanced on a high wire
weighed down from snowy pines—
a Jay in showy blue is watching

strings of mucous swing
from an old man's nose
like a trapeze

watching the sway,
watching, watching,
then flying away,

(leaving him alone)
here, on this street,

no net to catch the falling,
only snow.

At a Crossroads in Japan

Because it is not familiar
with US Patent 5296248—
a method for cracking walnuts
and recovery of nut meat therefrom—
the Carrion Crow waits
until yellow fades to red.

Then, before stopped traffic, it
saunters out with the sea of pedestrians
and with its blunt beak, nudges a walnut
—just so—in front of a rumbling tire,
then flies away.

Light turns red to green,
the cars move forward and
brown eyes watch safely from a distance
as the tire rolls over and crushes the nut.

When light returns to red,
glossy blackness swoops down.
In its green and purple robe of splendor
the crow, an invisible emperor
in this returning wave of people

hops before the once hidden delight.
Succulent meatiness
splayed upon a tarry platter,
there now for the taking.

From a Second Floor Verandah in Naples, Florida

Through a shower of
jewels—left behind
by fog—dripping from
thin, white arms
of pines,

he swings
and a *'crack'*
snaps
at the still
drowsy air of morning.

Lifting palm to brow,
he salutes his work,
fixes his gaze beyond.
His work here is done.

Emerging from
dappled green, he
steps into a white cart
puffs on a fat cigar
and drives away—

leaving behind
footprints,
soon erased
by a waking sun.

The Offender Recalls the First Time

He did it in the kitchen.

In the tidy room that mocked him—
with the faucet he couldn't turn,
refrigerator door he couldn't open,
where strawberries as big as fists
pounded out patterns onto curtains
he could not draw aside.

He chose the room where the girl lay
on her belly, feet dancing in the air,
as she played with her dolls.

His mother had left him alone for a time.

Keep an eye on your niece, she'd said.
Gotta run to the store.
Be back in two winks of an eye.

She was always saying that.
God, how he hated that expression—
and the lilt in her voice, as if everything
was fine—but he boomed out
a reassuring *will do* as she
headed out the door.

Uncle Lenny loves you
he would say
in a voice that would

melt her heart
and freeze it
all at once,

that instructed her
in the rules of secret play:
to remove

his sock and shoe and then
her princess panties
and lay herself upon the floor
—cold linoleum squares
connected by black diamonds—
(the shape of jagged tears
she would recall years later).

He felt so strong
as she lay silent,
still and small.

From his wheelchair
he would murmur
Uncle Lenny loves you
as his meaty toe
burrowed itself
inside her moist cave
and sighed.

Charleston's Circle Church Graveyard in Early March

Moss, like soft gray tears drips from the Magnolia's thick arms
whose fists have yet to bloom. At its feet

we slumber,
a smattering of virtuous consorts sharing a chiseled faith, undone by time,

tender parents, affectionate husbands (would we loyal wives agree?),
sullen children and days old infants tucked sweetly into earthen beds—

the span of years collapsed, as frail headboards huddle together,
a few refuse to press in, to seek company even in death.

Sweet Jesus, save us from this crumbled life.

The Neighbors Behind Me and Two Doors Down

Between us—rising from the earth—a mulberry tree,
a wooden fence, a clump of overgrown miscanthus,
volunteers of pink hollyhocks and swaying sunflowers.

Between growth both wild and sown,
I'd catch glimpses of your hair sprouting wild and white,
your crooked back bowed down,
seemingly without complaint, to greet and separate
weeds from flowers, to tend with care
your small slice of this world.

You would, at times, unfold your lanky body
and catch me, watching you.
Between growth both wild and sown,
you'd smile, one gloved hand holding weeds, the other waving.

From the start, we dismissed formality of names,
got right to the point about rains that had yet to fall,
what a bad year it was for tomatoes, or how next year,
you might plant more zinnias, I might divide the daffodils.
And then our hands would both return to dirt.

Your wife, without fail, would swing open the screen door,
and step out onto the porch with two glasses
of lemonade or water. She'd set them down,
wipe her hands on the apron tied around her waist,
and study your quiet ways.

When you were done, you'd sit
side by side, sipping drinks, gazing upon
your patch of heaven.

It is an October Saturday. A perfect
gardening day. Your wife, without
an apron, steps out onto the porch.
Between growth both wild and sown,
she shouts: *My husband died on Wednesday.*
Even though I don't know your name, I wanted you to know...

I do not know what to say and so I say,
I will miss seeing him in his garden.
Me too, she says.

That evening, from my bedroom window
I gaze upon your labor.
African Marigolds, sturdy and tall,
glow beneath the harvest moon.

Through window not yet drawn,
a light glows, exposing lace
curtains, blue walls. A figure
slowly crosses the room.
Between all things both wild and sown,
marigold faces shine, the bounty
of your hands reaches out to her.

Lives Overlapped

She does not want to break the chain
of knowing him so

to touch the past
each dog is obtained
while the current one lives.

May each, she prays, pass down
the memory of the first one:
a curled up, resting-in-his-lap memory,
upon ever thinning legs, covered in Haband pants
the man had ordered from Reader's Digest.

Enveloped in the cherry smell of his pipe and
lulled by the television's steady hum,
the dog observes lazily with one eye
as the man's lips form an O and
release puffs of cloudy, white rings;

the girl attempts to marry this moment,
reaches high above her head and slips
a tiny finger into already vanishing rings.

She does not want to break this chain
of knowing him.

Etymological Swim

Carried on the mighty backs
of ocean waves,
over thousands of miles
language drifts, eventually
tumbles to shore and—
battered from its journey,
is unrecognizable,
tangled in seaweed,
dripping with the waters
from which it came.

Upon Attending the Unveiling of Galaxy Messier 101

Between spaces of conversation
we orbit the mystery of each other,
dipping into a dash of comet, savoring a snack of star,
waiting to partake in a galactic meal of Messier 101.

We form a half moon, a quilt of eager bodies
pieced together and as the veil is lifted
hungry eyes feast upon a galaxy
as it looked and lived and breathed
22 million light years ago. Our eyes touched by

light that set forth on its journey to us,
just as the dinosaurs disappeared and the
Mastodon set its massive foot on earth,
this light from then only reaching us now.

The Hubble sees the visible, a whirling
pinwheel missing-its-stick galaxy
dipped in cotton candy, a fluffy center
drizzled in light caramel, arms swirling,
beckoning: come and taste.

Spitzer's infrared eye peers into a blue
haze and sees—warmed by the light of baby stars—
dusty red wombs, ready to spill life
into this eye-of-a-hurricane galaxy.

The Chandra's x-ray vision peers
into a sea of darkness, exposing the sparkling
head of a blue and red dandelion,
a mix of untold worlds gone to seed.

It takes three different telescopes to pull
together the final course,
three realities overlapping
to expose the essence of one galaxy.

It is as if we are
entering the eyes of God
to peel back time and dine on ancient beauty,
this lusty, exploding stew of color
and spiraling movement...

Stripped of all-seeing eyes
we orbit the mystery of each other
and leave, patting bellies
full of old universe, palates

eager and curious to taste
Messier *at this moment.* But we
must be patient, must wait
22 million years for light to reach us,
to show us today.

Apology to the Grayling

When the Michigan Department of Conservation declared: *our native grayling has followed the passenger pigeon and the heath hen into Limbo* half of me was in the Northern woods of Manistee, slumbering in the ovarian cave of a one year old child.

Grayling and grayling never to come, I apologize for us. I am a descendent of we the people who killed the goose who laid the golden egg. I am sorry you looked so fine, swam so strong, tasted so delicious…

Perhaps if you could have laid low, been less tempting a beauty both inside and out things might have turned out differently. I am not casting blame. I am not. I only want you to understand that when we hooked, fried and lied to you, cast nets with meshes smaller than laws allowed, and caught you before you had a chance to spawn, we did not realize that the rainbow and brook trout we placed in your home would nibble your children to death.

Forgive too my ignorance, not knowing the story of you, the genocide of your kind by my peoples' hands. One set of those hands belonged to my mother's mother's father. He was just trying to make a living. He was a hard drinking Irish logger who joined with others and slew majestic beasts, loyal, leafy soldiers who kept cool your waters. Slaughtered in their forest homes, a spring harvest of trees unleashed sediments as their giant bodies tumbled to their deaths. Your delicate grayling eggs were buried alive. Generations and generations not to come, suffocated under murky blankets.

All this apologizing and I have left the waiting room. I am somehow here, in the early 1800's, under the canopy of achingly tall trees with bellies big from 300 years of being. Into a stream hugged by juicy grasses, fish fall from the heavens. Grayling, sleek and graceful fly underwater. Thousands upon thousands shimmer and glide. Shimmer and glide. One stops and raises his head. His mouth doesn't move but he is talking all the same.

> *I am king of this river*, he says. Shimmer and glide.
> I have to laugh. To think that a fish believes he is a king.
> *It is true*, the trees whisper.
> *Drink*, says the grayling. Shimmer and glide.
> Hands cupped, I dip into his river offering. Fresh as first snowfall, the water is so pure it burns. It is all too much to take in.

I return to this waiting room, a world emptied of a king's existence. An old woman in a salmon colored sweater sits and waits. The only thing barely moving is her sagging lids closing and opening, closing and opening over milky eyes.

Looking for an anchor to keep me from drifting back again into the 1800's, I plunge my hands into a stack of magazines. My fingers hook onto *Field & Stream*, the August 2008 edition. Smiling men in various poses hold huge fish. Page 20 and 21 is a centerfold, titled "The Beautiful and the Damned." Splashed across its pages is an underwater picture of an obscenely beautiful fish. The coral belly glistens, speckles of black grace its tail and back. Unlike the men, the fish is not smiling. Its mouth droops as if anticipating its own demise. Montana's state fish, warns the magazine, a native trout, is becoming rare due to mining pollution.

I want to grab the salmon sweatered woman before she floats away, shout: *don't you see what is happening here?* But grayling, I just wait. Wait like I did 70 years ago when only half of me was here. This time, though, I am snared in one of your trees. I did not realize some of its branches had latched onto my mind and I unwittingly have brought the last of you through time with me. Tired of re-membering, the tree releases its offerings like swollen fruit into my hair.

Right here in this waiting room, where salmon woman now deeply sleeps, a mass of unborn eggs begin to hatch. Your brothers and sisters, a cousin once and twice removed, are all tangled up in this ridiculous, rather embarrassing gelatinous fishy hairdo. My fingers comb through knotted, grayed up hair. Fish fall out, flop at my feet. One sails across the room, smacks the beige wall with its wet tail, and slides down, dangerously close to the woman who has forgotten she is waiting for her name to be called, while you, grayling, land solemnly on my lap. There is only one thing to do. I swallow you whole; lick your iridescence from my lips.

Old friend, I shall never again see the likes of you. You have become a constant, nagging pressure—my left side to be exact, for you have slipped from your watery life, journeyed into the rough, barky soul of a tree that, weighed down by all that it has borne, has shed you into me.

I apologize if your new accommodations are a bit tight, but at least it is—a place.
I feel your scaly body press against my ribs, your tail flicks in anticipation against my spine; an eye peers out from behind my left kidney.

My dear grayling, the doctors won't find you. Just keep hiding. This world, which was not kind to you, is still not ready for such beauty.

"A bat that was clinging to space shuttle Discovery's external fuel tank during the countdown to launch the STS-119 mission remained with the spacecraft as it cleared the tower, analysts at NASA's Kennedy Space Center concluded.... It was not the first bat to land on a shuttle during a countdown...."

—Steven Siceloff, NASA's John F. Kennedy Space Center
Posted on NASA's website, 3/17/09

The Hard Ones' Response

You were seen as some broken,
stupid bat who didn't know
what he was doing.
Deemed too small
to be considered a debris risk,
NASA dismissed you
as a hapless stowaway
and shuttled off to the stars.
PETA protested with *Bats are people too!* signs.
For a short time, you were the
darling of a small, internet following.
The Hard Ones mistakenly thought
your death was about you.
They named you Brian.

"More than 50% of America's 47 bat species are in severe decline or already listed as endangered. Losses are occurring at alarming rates worldwide."

—Monique Smith-Lee, Native Animal Rescue Wildlife Rehabilitator

Interim Problem Report 119V-0080

This is the memo written:
Interim Problem Report 119V-0080,
by the NASA official who,
just before lift off, has observed you
clinging to the side of the space shuttle Discovery.

The mission you have accepted—self immolation—is underway.
Despite your injuries and the fact that you are
uncomfortable drawing attention to yourself
you hold on, you do not let go.

You think about why you can not fail, how
just weeks ago, against an acoustically cluttered sky
you and representatives from thousands
of other colonies gathered to resurrect a plan.

Because it was your father who failed back in '96
with the Endeavor and again in '98
with the Challenger, you volunteer,
despite your mother's pleas.

Your friends break your arm lest you
be tempted, as your father had been,
moments before launch, to fly away.

You take some comfort recalling the discussion that
protests have been lodged this way, that the two-legged,
hard-of-hearing creatures—the Hard Ones—
have used this plan themselves to bring attention

to wars, repressive regimes, atrocities unimagined.
Everyone wonders, why would someone go to this extreme?
It must be terribly important if a life sets fire to itself.
The Hard Ones know this elemental language and

will see you roosting where you should not; later
they will spot you clawing yourself
onto the foamy skin of the shuttle's external tank
and when they see you in flames,

the Hard Ones will finally know what your kind
has been crying out for years:
we bats are slipping from the sky—help us.

Because you are not your father,
you press your chest against the shuttle,
then turn and sweep the sky

10, 9, 8...
with mouth open wide you
emit the agreed upon ultrasonic call and
in the roar of engines, listen for reflected echoes.

7, 6, 5...
Your sonar pulses bounce off the closest of your kind.
Fuzzy pectoral breasts, aching and proud,
return to embrace you.
This is the physics of the heart,

4, 3, 2...
this is your mother.
she calls out to you one last time.
My brave, little hand-wing,
you are doing what your father could not...

1...
this is what your heart holds.
You listen. You hold on. You do not let go.
The Hard Ones are watching as
the shuttle tears itself from the earth.

Blast off...
This is what faith looks like: your tiny body,
covered in brownish gray fur, ignites,
you do not let go; this weight in grams
has never burned so bright.

I Find Myself

after being up since 4am with our child
and cooking blueberry pancakes,
serving up Saturday breakfast and watching
our son step gingerly to his chair
to navigate 'round shredded cheddar cheese
transformed by time into brittle shards of yellow glass,
listening to him wail—*there are too many crumbs on the floor,*
after clearing the table, rinsing dishes and filling the dishwasher,

I fling the dish towel over my pajama shoulders,
to bend and pick up peas that glisten
like tiny green land mines strewn amongst the jagged cheese,
then vacuum up the week. I feel the towel christen me
in cold, imagine tomorrow's headlines—*mother electrocuted:
crazy mishap with wet towel and vacuum.*

I find myself holding two containers
rinsed and ready for recycling in one hand,
cleaning the kitchen sink with the other,
and singing silently my praises—
look what I can do—and all before 9am.

A loud crash intrudes upon this self-adulation.
The vacuum cleaner has toppled over,
sending the cat—who had been orbiting my legs
like a drunken, fuzzy planet—scurrying out of the room.

My husband saunters in, a newspaper tucked under his arm.
He pours himself a second cup of coffee. Long legs prepare

to stretch over the vacuum, leaving it to rest
in the middle of the kitchen floor.

I clear my throat.
Could you please pick up the vacuum cleaner? Put it away?
He emits a small sigh. I read much into this tiny utterance.
It says: *Can't you leave me alone? You are too demanding.*
If you would have taken the time to wind up the cord
instead of heaping it on the side, it wouldn't have fallen down.

Over the horizon of his back,
for he is now leaning over the vacuum and
carefully wrapping the cord around the hooks,
I spot the coffee cup I abandoned and can not reach
until he moves. He is slow, meticulous.

Finally. I grab my coffee and search for a slice of space
which demands nothing of me; a chair in which I do not have to
remove a ball, a toy train, a book, a sippy, a Clifford slipper,
all which somehow mysteriously appeared as I was
busying myself in the kitchen.

I find myself uncomfortably on the verge of martyrdom.
To abscond from this kingdom in which I could easily reign,
I forego the undoneness of day—the unmade beds,
unbrushed teeth, unwashed clothes,
and write.

In taking time to write these words,
even something as mundane as three-day old cheese
and peas resting on the floor,

I find myself.

Allied in Spring

Spring is wires.
Twisted rows of rust
blossom on tips of tiny fists that refuse to unfurl
upon fences that sometimes frame,
sometimes focus in on

a woman's heart that beats relentlessly, beyond reach.
She offers up a barbed, bitter kind of love—
the kind that scrapes your insides raw,
leaves you bloody, hanging
wishing you had loved another.

While secrets buried
seep ever down as she grows weary,
you pretend that all is well—
see, upon her full body
skin emerges, juicy, green,

buds tight with promise swell, and there,
nestled at her side hope ripples, shines
then slips behind concrete muscles. Her
love unleashed drifts down
and into the Kalamazoo.

You can not avoid her, this dangerous woman,
living in the center of town. She is not safe to know,
but you can not leave her. She is your future, so you don't give up
until steely, knotted nerves unravel
and she stands before you empty, undone.

Til then,

you feel guilty for loving her
saying she is beautiful, even now
in this, her bloodied, tangled Spring.

Allied in Summer

Nature blamelessly knits
sweater of greens,

loose stitches laced with
hint of streaming water.

Draped in layers of
billowing garments

this saucy girl
stews in heat.

She barely
lets you see her,

you tell yourself
she is just fine.

Grieving the God of My Youth

I.

I was eleven or so
when He closed up shop,

dismantled the neon sign
that hung outside my bedroom window,
the one that never glowed:
You shall be a BALLERINA. Or,
Become an ASTRONAUT and fly to the moon. Or,
Your destiny is to RIDE HORSES by day
and EAT OREOS—just the creamy insides—by night.

He swung a musty, leather suitcase onto the foot of my bed,
snapped off his flowing, white beard, rolled it up 'til it looked
like a child's furry hand-muff and placed it inside.
Large hands then gripped the slender waist of my guardian angel (who, during
this time, had begun to hover less enthusiastically over my right shoulder),
she went to Him with such force that her halo came askew,
bits of glitter flew from her robe, twinkled to the floor.
He folded sparkly her up, taking care to tuck in delicate wings. Then
He pulled a tired-looking broom and dustpan—swept up
shimmery light that crunched like broken stars beneath His feet—and stuffed it all
into the suitcase. All packed up, He snapped the case closed
and slipped out the door.

Light, in the form of headlights
sped across bedroom walls,

swayed below the doorknob
and disappeared.

II. (Dead Jesus)

Around this time, the new priest took down our dead, wooden Jesus and put up another, the risen One. Suspended over the altar by two chains, this Risen Christ with child-like hands on full, outstretched arms, beckoned and was shunned by those who wanted their dead One back.

Too young to know any differently, I leapt and used the flowing metal body as stepping stones. My soul would stretch, take hold of tiny fingers and reach this swinging cross made just for me. Enfolded in Love, we'd sway unseen, above pews drowning in solemn faces.   See how the Spirit blows, lifts you up into the hands of Love. Come into this cross made just for you.

Grotesque, mrs. o'reilly whispered into her black glove. *A travesty* her friend agreed. Swinging high above their heads, we sang with joy, our breath stirred the air and still, they felt nothing. We were sad for them, so many wanting their dead Jesus back.
Years went by.
They missed the skin bleached by pain, the crown of tangled thorns that gripped the brow, nails pounded into flesh, the blood, the broken.
Grownups, I concluded, need their Jesus wounded. Dead weight, though, is so much harder to carry. How much they were missing, too afraid to set their dead One free.

III. (Dead Jesus Returns)

I was away at college when the new priest turned old. *Take your Christ with you*, the people told him. My mother told me this. She had always liked the Risen Christ. *A piece of art, it makes you think*, she'd said. I wondered: if she had been like them, preferred the eyes-closed-can't-hold-you-now-I'm-busy-dying-Jesus, would I have swung? She must have been a stepping stone.

I imagined the old priest carrying out his cross, on his back, the chains dragging behind him, no one to help.

Their Jesus returned and they nailed him up. Once again.

I Want a Church

I want to find me a church
where artisans of peace and justice
tired from practicing their craft
find themselves in pews which
break like waves against the altar,

waves that swell and stretch
anchors of all shapes and sizes,
washing those who have
gathered into this singing place
out again, far and wide
into unknown, dangerous waters.

I want a church
made of sailors who know
that it is not about the boat,
who resist the temptation
to stay on board
and play it safe
for fear of drowning,
or worse yet, that nets cast
will come up empty
and I, you, we will have nothing
to show for our efforts.

I want a church
that celebrates sailors
who step out of the boat
and with wobbly sea legs
stagger onto dry land

and find themselves
just brave enough to
chisel watery souls with love.

What I Wanted to Say

When you returned my Sunday call
left with your answering service and I told you
her pulse was erratic, blood pressure fluctuating wildly and
reminded you of her recent diagnosis of afibrillation
        what I wanted to say was
her heart can not hold another. I have only known
my mother's heart to be big enough to hold the sky.
To think of it as only one fluttery muscle in this vast world frightens me.

When you asked of other symptoms and I told you she was dizzy,
I should have told you that our world is spinning, that my sister
has driven across town and dragged into my parent's perfectly clean home
a vacuum cleaner, mop and host of cleaning supplies because
        she wants to do something,
it is the only way she knows to be of some assistance
as she is a comet burning, streaking across the living room
with her swiffer, saying *I just love this swiffer,
especially with the long handle attachment, do you have one?
I don't know how I ever managed to dust before
this invention and I couldn't find the long handle of mine
so I'm so glad I could find yours. Mom, you don't mind do you?*
My mother puts one hand to her head, the other hand
waves away this noisome child.
        When did my mother's hands grow old?

I wanted to mention that between beats my mother worries
that her husband isn't going to have a proper dinner. When she creaks out
oh, honey, I wanted to fix you that beautiful roast you bought the other day,
my sister stops with the swiffering and says *I'll fix the roast* and flies into
the kitchen

and we all—my mother, father, sister and me—breathe a sigh of relief that she could now safely orbit a chunk of meat.

When you asked about her dosage and I told you it was 25 mgs of Rhythmol, what I wanted to say was my father seems suddenly old and helpless, his hands shaking
as he tries to comfort his wife with pillows and food and pills, all which she is refusing.
She is swatting us away like gnats but we can't help but hover near her.
    We are drawn to her. She is our light.

Because it happened after we got off the phone, I couldn't report this to you but my sister, in the middle of preparing the roast, stopped and
demanded of my mother—*who did you call first?*
At the same time my sister said—*I live closer, you should have called me, why didn't you call me?*—my mother sighed: *your sister called me.*
    This immediately appeased my sister who
gravitated back to seasoning the roast.

When you paused I heard myself fill the silence, saying, *she just isn't herself.*
What I was trying to get across is that she is the type of woman who likes to be in control, who takes pride in not asking anything of others. Her phone rings steadily throughout the day with friends and acquaintances calling to obtain her advice or get her take on their ailments. So when she called and said *can you come over* I said *sure* and hung up the phone,
    leaving the mouth of the dryer opened wide in amazement,
clothes tumbling over themselves, spilling onto the floor and ran out the door and found her in the shower unable to step out.
I toweled her off like she did for me when I was little.
I helped her dress and watched her watching me as if somehow
I could make her better. So you've got to make her all better please.
    Fix her fix her fix her.

Then my sister can stop dusting,
my father can stop wringing his hands
and I can be her daughter again.

When we hung up, I don't think you heard me at all.

Even Heaven Will Not Be Like This

On this Sunday morning, in which
snow falls the size of saucers, we snuggle
in this chair built for giant men,
enveloped in the blanket you have
dragged downstairs. Miracles abound.

Your small body nestles into mine.
Peonies brazenly open to
chilly countenance of January
as your steam train chugs along
the cotton rails of my arm.

I kiss the top of your head, pose
this question: Will you come to me
when you are grown
and rest upon my lap?
Yes mamma, you reply in earnest.

Upstairs, a bed creaks, your father rises,
soon you will run to him. Coldness will
rush in to claim your spot.
Even this moment
is ending.

Laryngitis

I open mouth.
The larynx—that tiny
box nestled in hollow
of throat, packed with
confetti-like words and
streaming sentences
refuses to open up.

Words I want to say:
Did you sleep well?
      What do you want for breakfast?
Don't you tire of having dinosaur cereal
three weeks in a row?
      Did you brush your teeth?
Honey, will you be home for dinner?
      Do I look as pathetic as I don't sound?
burned up in this cavernous blaze.

Before my husband leaves for work,
he googles laryngitis,
ticks off what one should do
upon finding one's self without voice:
inhale steam, avoid clearing throat,
suck on lozenges, gargle salt water,
sip ginger root tea,
none of which I am doing.

He heads out the door with our son.
Take care of yourself, he says.

Because the soul does not speak in sentences
I stand
in ashes of unspoken
and wave goodbye.

Making Raspberries

I lay upon this bed, a sea,
and you, like a tiny boat
dock next to me,

kneel and thrust up
your chin, buoyantly
gulping in air.

With eyes wide open
and mouth in full sail
you pitch forward. Red lips

discover soft flesh
of land and release
sweet sputterings.

Again and again
you breathe in,
crash into me, until

you pull up anchor
speed away, leaving
a shimmering path

made wet and holy
in this attempt
to perfect your art.

Gay in the Age of Copper

(2900-2500 B.C.)

It is good to be gay
in this age of copper
where hope rises
over mountains
of crumbling flesh,

before bronze peeks its
heavy head over the horizon,
causing tools to harden, gives
way to iron horses and
weapons that can not be undone.

How good to be gay
in this age of copper,
curled by your people,
tucked into earth's womb
in honor of how you first arrived.

ii.

His people bury him
like they bury their women,
placing a simple pot at his feet
after they have readied his body
for the next life, posing his shape

just so, on his left side.
They turn his head east

and stretch the earth over him.
He, like the women, shall see thousands
upon thousands of days begin—

unlike their men—
buried with hammers,
weapons, knives of flint.
Facing west, these men know
when the world slips away.

iii.

The wisdom of this age
is in us now, in our liver,
our bones, our blood. You'd

think that all these
patinated platelets coursing
through rivers of veins

would make us a species
highly conducive to living light
on this munificent land.

iv.

It is only a matter of time
before we return
to the mouths
of hungry caves.

What the Balloon Saw

The boy does not rise,
stands like stone, face
pointed at the sky when

the speck of a father
sweeps him up and
together they

fade away. White
chunks of land shift,
continents melt away

blue coldness ripples,
empties into a vast sea
of darkness where

colossal balloons
without tails
surface on occasion.

Earth's breath buoys
thin-skinned hope
through time, to the

fringe of the Milky
Way where a dazzling,
clustered colony of

jeweled orbs
encircles a giddy planet,

whence it considers

the boy's
spiral galaxy
edge on,

a cookie dunked in
milk—1,000 light years
thick—then, releasing

a small sigh, puts
down its string with
countless others

blown together
by this dance of
lost memories.

In The Downpour of Your Absence

                              u   y   o   u
                           o
                        Y
                        O
                        U
                        You
                    were my roof.
              So, when you up and left
            me and the kids without even leaving
          so much as a shingle, I'd lay awake at night,
          missing the gentle slope of you, bared to the naked
        sky, nothing to stop me now from touching the burning stars,
yanking them down, crushing them like ice between my teeth. The impossible
was here. In exposing the rooms of us to the elements of ancient moon and dust
                    you flung   open

                a widow   and
everything night rushed into me and spilled upon the children.
Dusk poured into your cereal bowl that sat on the counter —
  shadows sloshed into the entryway where your boots leaned
            against themselves.   Everything day
    seared us.   We baked in memory.   Your hat hung on the
    hook where   you   last   left it—reminding
    us of the bigger brim of you.   It became dangerous to walk
    floors slick with heaven's clutter.   The kids began resenting
    the daily chore of raking leaves that crumbled like broken fists
                upon the kitchen table. Then
              winter arrived and for weeks at a times
    we couldn't find each other.   I dug a path to the door,
    the kids helped me.   You   would have been proud
    of them. They worked really   hard.   Eventually,
                              we
                             had
                              to
                          move on.

In Trying to Find a Home for Your Jewelry

Before you die, you might—even though
you aren't a particularly warm person—
feel the need to press a chunky
silver bracelet into the palm of a woman
you hardly know—say simply,
I want you to have this,
think, but do not utter: *to remember me by,*
not knowing that when you have slipped away
it will be worn faithfully for years
until its tarnished skin leaves a stain,
a banded bruise around the wrist,
and it becomes lost, right along with your last name,
the name you did not pass down
because you never married or had children.

Uncle Ernie's Pancake House, Labor Day

The waitress pours a cup
of joe, works her way around
long-eared men, doused in flannel
on this day that dips below 70 degrees;
a pair of watery eyes hinges
on the one with fleshy lips
droning on about where to find

used snow plows on sale and how
Sweet Belle surprised him by up and
dying in '95—the same year he planned to
retire but didn't because he thought
what's the point now?

Yep, yep, yep, one whirrs in response,
his last bit of toast stalled
like a charred plane
hovering over easy clouds.
Sun breaks through, bleeds into white.
Conversation sputters, toast quivers
then disappears, yep, yep.

In crowded skies, movements of old men
cast shadows at alarming rates; elbows
touching down on runways
strewn with napkins, buttered crumbs
brushed from washed out whiskers;

well-traveled crafts
nosing in for final descent,
formica strips made shiny
by those who have come before.
Yep, yep.

In This Time of Drought a Silver Lining

In this place shed of watery skins
sleepy towns awaken, streets yawn open,
their parched tongues paved in cotton gins,
arrow heads, cow bones, and wagon wheels.

Sealed lips split as the graves of slaves rise up,
sunken ships surface, a booty of beer cans
and missing bodies rattle about as ribbed vessels
hold steady upon hardened waves
of sand, once grass, once water.

Here, on this splintered earth
one place becomes another.
That which remains thirsts
to no longer feel its weight.

The Molting Season

Time has a way of melding
recurring moments into one, like
that Saturday my father gathered me up
with books and papers and took me

to work with him, let me wander his lab,
past countertops unruffled by rows
of sinks sunk into sterile bellies.
Swan-necked faucets rose haughtily

over microscopes and beakers, snubbing
the giant king crab that adorned the wall.
Beneath suspended claws, aquariums bubbled
a tarantula tank hummed, then came

the brutal beauty of butterflies pursued,
a mélange of delicate wings splayed
under glass as a shiny chorus of pins sang
to no one in particular or to flocks

of students who took note of his discourse,
caught in their papery nets words like
exoskeleton, thorax, and
ecdysis.

Two generations of cicadas later
it's disconcerting he could tell no one—
not his wife who found him, paramedics
who arrived on the scene, the E.R. doctors

who stitched him up, or his grown children
who kept asking—how it came to be
he opened himself up
upon the hardness of the bathroom floor.

        He has grown
           too big for this world, has shrugged off
           his inner suit, shed rusted wings and
burrowed himself into fine places.

Armed with only a rag, I am
unable to pin down,
just out of reach, my father
tumbling away from me.

Genealogy Goes Both Ways on Park Street

I trail on foot, his bicycle
freshly shorn of training wheels.

My son traverses his maternal line,
moored to maples whose heavy heads
douse us in shade,

whose tangled feet yawn beneath us,
heaving up in places, nudging
those who forget
into remembering.

Spring after spring has passed
and yet, new blooms alight
upon the same flock of lilac bushes,
anointing air in heady hope
traced back decades.

Ivy sleeves of chimney arms
wave as my boy breezes by house after house.
There is the golden quarters
someone has painted a solemn blue.

And here, right here I took piano lessons
behind diaphanous drapes where a spider plant—
babies of the babies babies—
tumbles from a macramé planter hanger.

                    To think,
she still has that fibrous rope of juted jazz,
with smooth, wooden beads I gave her—
one of many made the winter of 1977.

Night after night, I tell him,
your grandma let me stay up late
to watch Alex Hailey
unravel his African roots.

As LeVar Burton played Kunta Kinte
my hands braided blue notes,
jangled knots until the rope twisted,
swung with restless sounds.

I abandoned common chords,
took up the notion—
history hangs together.

Fingers, raw with the rhythm,
would leave traces of blood
on the ivory keys of a woman
who stopped offering
lessons years ago,

now a hunched shadow,
stooped over her dining room table
folding napkins or a letter.

A Brief Notion in the Evolution of Avian Migration

To think, that birds
would hibernate like bears,
hunkered down in muddied waters

having gathered at banks
of marshes, locked scaly toes
'round reeds, until hollowed

heaviness bent stalks and the
passerines slipped under—veiled
in silt, submerged 'til Spring,

when they would rise, return
to dress the skies but not before
a few fishermen bragged

they had drawn nets
brimming with drowsy
swallows, wings sodden

with sleep.
No wonder this notion
persisted; it's comforting

to think that beauty
doesn't really
leave us,

that one's final
destination is just a
pond away.

CPSIA information can be obtained at www.ICGtesting.com
Printed in the USA
LVOW11s2202020516

486311LV00006B/822/P